R. L. SCOTT-BUCCLEUCH

The Promise

MACMILLAN READERS

ELEMENTARY LEVEL

Founding Editor: John Milne

The Macmillan Readers provide a choice of enjoyable reading materials for learners of English. The series is published at six levels – Starter, Beginner, Elementary, Pre-intermediate, Intermediate and Upper.

Level control

Information, structure and vocabulary are controlled to suit the students' ability at each level.

The number of words at each level:

Starter	about 300 basic words
Beginner	about 600 basic words
Elementary	about 1100 basic words
Pre-intermediate	about 1400 basic words
Intermediate	about 1600 basic words
Upper	about 2200 basic words

Vocabulary

Some difficult words and phrases in this book are important for understanding the story. Some of these words are explained in the story and some are shown in the pictures. From Pre-intermediate level upwards, words are marked with a number like this: ...³. These words are explained in the Glossary at the end of the book.

Contents

1

The Promise

Bahia is a state in Brazil. Many of Brazil's greatest poets and writers were born in Bahia. Tourists come to Bahia from all over the world. They play on the sandy beaches and they swim in the water of the Atlantic.

More than a million people live in Salvador, the capital of Bahia. Some of them are very rich and live in large houses. They have motor cars and servants. Others are not so rich, but they have work and live in small houses. There are many more who are very poor. They live in little wooden huts.

Pedro Moreira lived in a hut on a hillside. The hill was called Gloria. Pedro lived with his wife, Maria. Their hut had only one small room which was almost empty. There was only an old table, a broken chair and a mattress.

CARIBBEAN SEA

Maria brought water from a spring which was more than a kilometre away.

One day, Pedro was sitting on the ground outside his hut. He was looking very unhappy. His wife was going to have a baby. They had had three other children before, but they had all died. Pedro wanted a son. But how could he get food for a new baby?

A woman passed by and spoke to him.

'Any news yet, Pedro?' she asked.

'Not yet, Teresa,' replied Pedro.

'It will be a boy this time,' said Teresa. 'I'm sure of that.'

'It doesn't make any difference,' replied Pedro. 'What will he eat? I have no work and no money.'

'Things will be better tomorrow,' said Teresa. 'Don't lose hope.'

Pedro did not reply. He sat quietly for more than an hour.

Finally, there was a noise inside the hut. An old woman came out. She was carrying a new-born baby. It was small, thin and ugly and it was crying loudly.

'Here, Pedro,' said the old woman. 'You have a son.' The old woman put the baby in Pedro's arms. Pedro looked at his son for a long time.

'Tell me something,' he said at last to the old woman. 'Will the baby live?'

The old woman did not reply immediately. She took the baby from Pedro. She closed her eyes and held the baby in her arms. Then she spoke. 'Yes,' she said, 'this boy will live.'

Pedro felt better. He believed this old woman. The old woman was nearly a hundred years old. She had come with her parents from Africa many years ago. She was able to cure sick people. Some people said that she was able to see into the future. She was always sent for when a baby was born.

'Listen, Pedro,' she said. 'I have more to tell you.'

Her face had a strange look and Pedro listened in silence.

'This boy will grow up and become famous,' she continued. 'He will be well-known all over the world. He will give happiness to many people.'

Some neighbours were standing near Pedro's hut. They were watching and listening. The old woman held up the baby and showed it to the neighbours.

'This baby will become a great man,' she said. 'One day, he will be rich. He will give happiness to many people and he will help poor people like us.'

Pedro looked at the neighbours. None of them laughed. They all believed the old woman and they were afraid of her.

The old woman went back into the hut and gave the baby to Maria. The old woman came out again and spoke to Pedro.

'This boy will grow up and become famous. He will give happiness to many people.'

'Perhaps you do not believe me,' she said, 'but I never make a mistake. Your son will come near to death many times, but do not lose hope. Remember my words and take good care of him. Be a good father to the boy. One day, he will be a good son to you. That is my promise.'

2

The Family

Pedro and Maria often remembered the words of the old woman. The baby was called Paulo. And after Paulo, they had no more children.

Pedro was not able to find a job. Sometimes he found work for a few days. He worked as a porter or washed dishes in a restaurant. Maria made a little money. She washed and mended clothes. The work was hard and people did not pay her much money.

Food was expensive and Pedro and Maria were always hungry. Paulo was hungry too. He cried all the time. He was small and thin and weak, but he did not die.

For a long time, Paulo stayed inside the hut. After three years, he was able to go outside and play with other children. His arms and legs were very thin. His legs were twisted. The other children called him Palito – a thin stick. And he was called Palito for the rest of his life.

One day, Pedro came running home.

'Maria, Maria,' he shouted. 'I've got a job.'

'A job?' asked Maria. 'Where?'

'With the bus company,' replied Pedro. 'I'm going to be a bus driver. Now we shall have enough money for food.'

Pedro worked twelve hours a day as a bus driver. The wages were not good, but he was happy. He was paid his wages every month and every pay day he came home with a large parcel of food. His family were never hungry again.

One evening, Pedro came home late. He had two young girls with him.

'Palito,' he called. 'Come and meet your cousins.'

Palito ran to his father and looked at the girls.

'This is Fernanda,' said Pedro. 'And this is Odete. They're your cousins and they're coming to live with us.'

Palito was nine years old now. He was pleased to meet the other children. They all shook hands and walked up the hill to the hut.

Fernanda was the same age as Palito, but she was much taller. She was a very pretty girl and walked proudly. Odete, her sister, was two years younger. She was pretty too, but she was shy. She cried all the time and covered her face with her hands.

The two girls had lived in another town with their parents. Their hut had caught fire and their parents were dead. Their mother was Pedro's sister. Now they were coming to live with Pedro and Maria and Palito. They were soon like one family.

Pedro sent all the children to school. Palito was not a good student. He did not like to study, but Fernanda and Odete helped him.

He learnt to read and to write quite well. Fernanda learnt very quickly, but she soon forgot her lessons. The best student was Odete. She studied hard and remembered her lessons.

Every day after school, Palito played football with the other boys. They usually played football for an hour. After that, they swam in the sea and rested in the sunshine. Then they played football again until dark. Palito's legs were still twisted, but they grew thicker and stronger.

Palito enjoyed these games. At first, the other boys knocked him over. But slowly he became more skilful. He learnt to turn quickly and carry the ball past the other boys. People often stopped and watched him playing.

He learnt to turn quickly and carry the ball past the other boys.

Sometimes Fernanda and Odete went to the beach with Palito. They watched him playing football. But usually the two girls had to stay with Maria. Pedro had bought an old sewing machine and Maria made clothes for rich ladies in the town.

Odete helped her and became very good at sewing. But Fernanda did not like sewing and she was very careless. Fernanda took the clothes to the houses of rich people. Because she was very pretty, people gave her more work. She took the work back to Maria and Odete. They were always busy.

Pedro was now a happy man. He was still poor, but he had work and his family had enough to eat.

Palito grew bigger and the neighbours began to talk about him.

'Look at Palito,' they said. 'He's a man now. Why isn't he working?'

Pedro smiled, but he did not reply. He went to the beach every Sunday and watched his son playing football.

'You know, Maria,' he said to his wife one Sunday evening, 'I've been watching Palito carefully. He's really good. He's going to be a footballer.'

3

Palito is Offered a Job

Pedro never forgot the words of the old woman.

How can I help Palito? he often asked himself. He isn't a good student. He'll never be a doctor or a teacher. But he is good at football.

One day Pedro had an idea. Because he was a bus driver, Pedro was a member of the Transport Workers' Club. The club had its own football team, called Corinthians. The bus company was proud of its team. The team players did not have to work much. They spent most of their time practising football.

Pedro spoke to the manager of the bus company. On his fifteenth birthday, Palito got a job with the company. He became a member of the Transport Workers' Club. Six months later, he was playing football for Corinthians. Palito played on the right wing because he could run so fast.

Every Sunday afternoon, Palito went to the City Stadium with his father. They watched the professional players carefully.

'Watch the wingers,' Pedro told his son. 'They stop the ball first. Then they pass the ball across the field to the strikers. Wingers don't score many goals. That's not their job. The strikers score the goals.'

Palito watched the professionals and he trained hard. He became more skilful. He dodged past other players and took the ball up the field. He tricked his opponents cleverly. The spectators laughed and cheered. His opponents became angry. They tried to kick Palito or catch his shirt. Palito learnt to dodge even more cleverly and his opponents were not able to catch him.

More people came to watch Corinthians. They wanted to see Palito play. His name became well-known in Bahia. The following year, Corinthians won the amateur championship. Palito's photograph was in the newspapers.

Palito was now seventeen. He was going to be a professional footballer. There was no doubt about that.

One day Palito came home very excited. He had a letter in his hand.

'Mum, Dad, look!' he shouted. 'I've got a letter. It's from the manager of Bahia Central.'

Bahia Central was one of the main teams in Bahia. The manager wanted Palito to play for Bahia Central. He was offering Palito a job.

Maria threw her arms round her son. Fernanda and Odete clapped their hands. They danced round the table and kissed Palito. Pedro did not say anything. He sat silently in his chair.

'What's wrong, Dad?' asked Palito. 'Aren't you pleased?'

'Of course, I'm pleased,' replied Pedro. 'But is this the best thing? Are you going to accept this first offer?'

'Not the best thing!' shouted Maria. 'Why not? Palito will be happy. He'll be rich.'

'Palito must accept,' said Fernanda.

There was silence for a moment. Then Odete spoke.

'What do you mean, Uncle?' she asked.

Pedro did not reply to the women. He looked straight at his son.

'Palito, where do all the best players in Brazil play?' he asked.

'In Rio and in São Paulo, of course,' replied Palito.

Maria threw her arms around her son.

'And when Brazil plays another country,' said Pedro, 'where do the players in that team come from?'

'From Rio and São Paulo,' replied Palito.

'How many Bahia players have ever played for Brazil?'

Palito thought for a few moments. 'I can't think of any,' he said.

'That's right,' said Pedro. 'Play for a Bahia team and you will never play for Brazil.'

'Palito! Play for Brazil!' shouted the two girls.

'Me? Play for Brazil?' asked Palito in surprise.

'Why not?' replied Pedro. 'You're good enough. You need more experience and you need training. One day, you'll play for Brazil. That is the greatest ambition of my life.'

'What's your advice then, Dad?' asked Palito.

'Ask the manager of Bahia Central to wait,' said Pedro. 'Don't refuse the offer immediately. Ask him to wait.'

Palito thought quietly for some time. Then he gave his decision.

'OK, Dad,' he said. 'You know best. I'll ask him to wait.'

4

Claudio's News

Palito wrote to Bahia Central's manager and the manager agreed to wait. Also, Pedro had a long talk with a friend of Palito's. This friend was called Claudio. He worked as a journalist for a newspaper.

A week later, there was a photograph of Palito on the sports page of the newspaper. Above the photograph were the words:

CENTRAL MAKE OFFER FOR YOUNG
CORINTHIANS' STAR

And under the photograph, there was an article about Palito. Claudio had written the article.

'Palito is good now,' wrote Claudio. 'In the future, he will be better. One day, he will be the best footballer in Brazil.'

Pedro came home early that evening. He was carrying ten copies of the newspaper. He had also bought ten large envelopes.

'Fernanda, Odete,' shouted Pedro, 'come here! I want your help.'

The two girls hurried in.

'Fernanda,' said Pedro, 'I have a job for you. Cut this article out of the newspapers. And you, Odete, you have the best handwriting. You can address the envelopes. I'll tell you the addresses.'

They worked together all evening. The next morning, Pedro put the ten envelopes in the post. They were addressed to the managers of the ten best teams in Rio

and São Paulo. In each envelope, there was a copy of the article about Palito.

Everybody on Gloria soon heard about the envelopes. They all waited for news.

'The team managers will fly here immediately,' Fernanda told Odete. 'They will offer Palito a job in Rio or in São Paulo.'

But nothing happened. Weeks passed and no news came.

'You're a fool, Palito,' some of his friends told him. 'Take the job with Bahia Central.'

Palito just smiled.

'Wait and see,' he told his friends.

Palito was busy training for an important match. Corinthians were going to play against Recife Rangers. This match was played every year and thousands of spectators came to watch. The match was always played in the City Stadium.

The evening before the match, Palito was sitting at home. He was talking to his father. Suddenly the door was thrown open and Claudio rushed into the room. He took Palito's arms and pulled him to his feet. Then he danced round and round the room with Palito.

'What's happened, Claudio?' shouted Pedro.

Claudio stopped dancing and looked at Pedro and Palito.

'News!' he said. 'Wonderful news!'

Fernanda, Odete and Maria had come into the hut.

'What news?' shouted Fernanda. 'Tell us the news.'

'Chico Perez is flying here tomorrow,' replied Claudio. 'He's the manager of White Star. He wants to see Palito play.'

'White Star?' asked Maria. 'What's that?'

'White Star is a team in São Paulo,' replied Claudio. 'They used to be the best team in Brazil. White Star used to be one of the best teams in the world.'

'That was ten years ago,' said Pedro. 'They're not so good now'

'That's true,' agreed Claudio. 'But Chico Perez is their new manager. He's trying to make them a great team again. He's looking for new, young players. He's already found a goalkeeper and a striker. Now he's looking for a winger.'

For a moment nobody spoke. They were all too surprised. Maria spoke first.

'And Chico Perez is coming to Salvador tomorrow,' she said.

'That's right,' said Claudio. 'He's coming here to see Palito. Do you know what I think, Maria? I think that tomorrow is going to be an important day in the history of Brazilian football.'

5

Corinthians v. Recife Rangers

The next day, the stadium was crowded. Thousands of spectators were singing and waving flags.

'Corinthians . . . Corinthians,' they were shouting. And then, 'Pa-li-to . . . Pa-li-to.'

Corinthians won the toss and the game began. The Recife team already knew about Palito and two defenders were marking him closely. The ball came to the right wing a number of times, but Palito could not pass these defenders. Each time he moved a few metres, stopped, and passed the ball back to the centre.

Then Corinthians nearly scored on the left wing. Recife moved one of the defenders away from Palito. Now he was able to run forward more easily.

The ball came to Palito and he ran with it up the field. A tall defender rushed at him. Palito stopped, turned quickly, and then ran on again. The defender fell and the crowd laughed and cheered.

Another Recife defender moved towards Palito. Palito cleverly kicked the ball between the defender's legs and ran on up the field. He looked up and saw a Corinthian striker in front of goal. Quickly, Palito passed the ball and the striker shot hard, straight at goal. The goalkeeper dived low but the ball went under him, into the net.

All round the stadium, the Corinthians' supporters cheered and shouted. A goal for Corinthians – after twenty minutes! Three more times in the first half, Palito ran up the field with the ball. He dodged past the Recife defenders and the crowd cheered.

He dodged past the Recife defenders and the crowd cheered.

The last time, he passed the ball straight to a Corinthian striker. The striker kicked hard. It was a beautiful shot, but the ball went straight into the arms of the goalkeeper.

The Recife goalkeeper moved quickly. He kicked the ball far up the field to a striker. The Recife striker stopped the ball and kicked it low and hard.

A goal for Recife! Recife 1, Corinthians 1. As the Recife supporters cheered, the whistle went for half-time.

In the second half, Corinthians attacked immediately. Every Recife player was defending. The Recife goalkeeper was everywhere. Twice the ball hit the crossbar, but Corinthians did not score.

Ten minutes passed. Fifteen minutes. Twenty minutes. The players became more and more nervous. The crowd was excited and impatient.

Then the ball came to Palito. A defender ran in front of Palito and he stopped. The defender stopped too and watched Palito. The ball lay on the ground between them.

Palito moved to his left, then to his right. The defender jumped one way, then the other. The crowd were enjoying themselves. They laughed and cheered.

Finally, Palito kicked the ball forward and ran round the Recife player. The angry defender caught Palito's shirt and pulled him back. The referee's whistle blew – a free kick to Corinthians.

Palito did not wait a second. He took the free kick – a high shot in front of the Recife goal. A Corinthians striker jumped in the air and headed the ball past the goalkeeper into the net. Another goal for Corinthians!

There was a tremendous noise in the stadium. Fireworks exploded and the Corinthians' supporters danced and

The angry defender caught Palito's shirt and pulled him back.

cheered. The Recife supporters sat silent.

The game began again and Recife now tried to attack. They wanted a draw but the game was nearly over. There was only five minutes left. Three minutes. Then two.

The last goal came suddenly. A bad pass from a Recife player gave the ball to Palito on the right wing. He was unmarked and ran up the field with the ball. Suddenly there was an open space between him and the goal. Palito did not pass the ball, but kept running.

The Recife goalkeeper saw the danger and moved out quickly. Behind him, the goal was empty. Palito waited for the right moment. He gently kicked the ball over the goalkeeper into the net.

A few seconds later, the referee blew his whistle and the game was over. Corinthians had beaten Recife by three goals to one.

'Palito . . .' the crowd sang. 'Pa-li-to . . .'

The Corinthians' players carried Palito on their shoulders round the field. Corinthians had won. Palito had made it possible.

After the match, the Corinthians' supporters sang and danced in the streets. There were many parties that night in Salvador. On Gloria, where Palito lived, the people lit fires and sang songs and danced. All night they talked about Palito. For them, Palito was the best football player in the world.

6

White Star

The next day Palito met Chico Perez. Chico asked him only one question.

'Your legs are all right, aren't they?' said Chico.

'Yes, they're all right,' replied Palito. 'They're twisted and they look funny. But they're strong.'

'Good,' said Chico Perez. 'Are you ready to come to São Paulo?'

'Of course,' replied Palito.

'Then you've got a job with White Star.'

Three weeks later the whole family arrived in São Paulo. They were given a small house. It had electric light and running water in the kitchen and bathroom. They had never seen such a fine house before.

Pedro got a job with Senhor Castro. Senhor Castro was the President of White Star and he owned three cars. Pedro became Senhor Castro's driver.

Fernanda and Odete got jobs too. They worked as servants for Senhora Castro, Senhor Castro's wife. Maria brought her sewing machine with her from Salvador. She made dresses for Senhora Castro and her friends.

Palito worked hard. The team met early every morning. They did physical exercises for an hour. Then the team practised with the ball. Every morning they finished with a quick game of football.

Palito soon got to know all the players in White Star. He made two special friends. Antonio was the main striker of the team. He was one year older than Palito. Antonio had joined White Star only a few months before.

Now he was playing for their first team. Antonio was able to kick the ball with great force. But he did not use his feet much. He scored more goals with his head than with his feet.

Palito also made friends with Waldir, the right back. Waldir was thirty-three years old. He had played for White Star for many years. He had played for them when they were the best team in Brazil.

Palito worked closely with Antonio and Waldir. They taught him a lot about football. Soon Palito was ready to play for the first team.

The day came for Palito's first big game. Chico Perez did not expect a large crowd. The White Star stadium held fifty thousand spectators. In the old days it had always been full. Now it was always more than half empty. The stands needed repairs and needed painting, but White Star had no money.

Chico wanted to see more spectators in the stadium. But first, White Star had to play better football. Then there would be more spectators and more money. Chico had brought Palito and Antonio and other young players to White Star. He was hoping for better football and bigger crowds.

Almost fifteen thousand spectators came to Palito's first game. Waldir, Antonio and Palito worked closely together. The other team were unable to stop them. The first goal was scored after only four minutes, the second goal after ten minutes. The final score was eight goals to nil.

That night the White Star supporters were happy. They sang and danced in the streets of São Paulo. White Star was becoming a great team again. The other players carried Palito and Antonio round the field on their shoulders.

Palito played for the first team for the rest of the season. White Star played fifteen more games. They won ten, drew three and lost two. Now forty thousand spectators watched White Star every Sunday.

Pedro watched all the games. He listened to the cheers of the crowd. They were cheering his son. Pedro felt a proud man.

Fernanda and Odete usually went to the games with Pedro.

'Palito's getting better all the time,' he told them one day. 'I'm sure that he'll play for Brazil next year.'

7

Troubles Begin

Palito was becoming richer. He bought a new house for himself and his family. It was a large, comfortable house near the White Star football ground. Pedro was still Senhor Castro's driver and Maria still made dresses. But Fernanda and Odete had new jobs. They did not work for Senhora Castro any more.

Fernanda had learnt to use make-up. She now worked for television and film companies. Her job was to put the make-up on the faces of actresses. She was good at her job and she was busy all the time.

Palito hoped to marry Fernanda one day. But she was changing. She worked hard and she wanted to become rich. Palito did not see her very often.

Odete had a job too. She worked for Dr Silveira – a well-known children's doctor in São Paulo. Children are often afraid of doctors. Odete kept the children happy while they were waiting to see Dr Silveira.

Palito had a short holiday. Then work began again. Palito trained hard with Antonio and Waldir. They played better than ever.

White Star began the new season well. They won the first five games. Every time the ball came to Palito's feet, the crowd cheered and shouted. Waldir was always behind Palito. And Antonio was in front of him. They made a perfect triangle. No one was able to beat them.

But Chico Perez was worried about Palito's legs. They were becoming more twisted. One day Chico spoke to Palito.

'The team doctor's here today. Let him have a look at your legs.' The doctor examined Palito's legs carefully.

'You're right,' the doctor said to Chico. 'His legs are becoming more twisted. They must be X rayed.'

'Is there any danger?' Chico asked the doctor.

'Don't make Palito work too hard,' replied the doctor. 'Don't ask him to play in every game.'

Palito was given a rest for a few weeks. He did not play in one or two unimportant games. But the White Star supporters wanted to see Palito. When Palito was not in the team, the supporters shouted out:

'Pa-li-to . . . Pa-li-to. We want Palito.'

Palito's legs were X-rayed. The bones were twisted, but the doctor did not find anything seriously wrong. Chico asked Palito to play again.

Palito played well in every game. The season was nearly over and White Star were third in the League Table. The next season, they hoped to win the League. Palito was now famous all over Brazil. Millions had seen him on television. His twisted legs had danced through defenders time after time.

Palito's name was in every newspaper. The newspapers said that he was going to be chosen for the Brazilian team. Pedro had been right. Palito was going to play for Brazil.

The season was nearly over. White Star had one more game to play. In this last game, White Star was playing a much weaker team.

By the end of the first half, White Star were winning three goals to nil. In the second half, Palito was playing brilliantly. He tricked the same defender time after time. The crowd laughed and cheered Palito. The defender became more and more angry.

Near the end of the game, Palito tricked the defender once again. The crowd laughed. The defender turned round and ran straight at Palito. He kicked Palito hard on the legs. Palito fell to the ground and lay still.

The referee immediately sent the defender off the field. The crowd shouted and whistled. Palito did not get to his feet. The team doctor ran out onto the field. Palito was carried off on a stretcher and taken straight to hospital.

8

The Operation

Chico and the team doctor went with Palito to the hospital. On the way, Palito told them the truth. His legs had been painful for some time. He had not wanted to disappoint Chico or the spectators. He had played in every important game. But he had often felt pains in his legs.

At the hospital, Palito's legs were X-rayed once again. And he was examined by a specialist. He was put in a bed in the hospital and Chico and the team doctor sat beside him. They waited for some time. Then the specialist came in with the X-ray photographs.

'What do you think, doctor?' Chico asked the specialist immediately.

'Palito must have an operation,' replied the specialist.

The specialist showed the X-ray photographs to the team doctor. The team doctor studied them carefully for some moments.

'Yes, I agree with the specialist,' the team doctor told Chico. 'Palito must have an operation immediately.'

Palito lay silent on the hospital bed. He was in great pain and he was not able to think clearly.

'What's wrong with Palito's legs?' asked Chico.

'It's something that happens to many poor children,' replied the specialist. 'Palito didn't have enough to eat when he was a baby. The bones in his legs didn't grow hard. They became twisted. Palito has been playing too much football. It's been too great a strain for his legs. He must have the operation or he'll never play football again.'

'What will happen in the operation?' asked Chico.

'We'll break the bones in Palito's legs,' replied the specialist. 'Then we'll set them again carefully. After some time, the bones will grow together again. And this time, they'll grow straight.'

Chico turned to Palito in his bed.

'Do you want to have this operation, Palito?' he asked.

Palito did not reply for some time because he was still in pain.

'When will I play football again?' he asked Chico.

Chico looked at the team doctor. The team doctor turned to the specialist.

'How long do you think?' said the team doctor.

'I don't know,' replied the specialist. 'Perhaps after three months. But it'll probably be much longer.'

'You won't be able to play for Brazil this year,' Chico told Palito. 'But you're young. You'll have many more chances later. It's better to have the operation now.'

Palito lay silent for a few moments.

'All right, Chico,' he said at last. 'You know best. I'll have this operation as soon as possible.'

Three days later, Palito was back in the hospital bed. Both his legs had been broken. They were covered with thick plaster casts and they were fixed to wires above his bed.

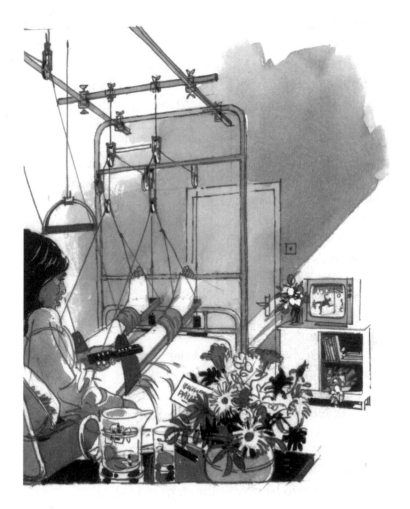

9

Fernanda

Every day, lots of Palito's friends came to the hospital. They brought him flowers, sweets and magazines. Palito talked to his visitors and looked at the magazines. He watched every football game on television. But he felt bored and impatient.

Antonio had been chosen to play for Brazil and he was training hard. Waldir had not been chosen because he was too old. He was still playing for White Star. Palito wanted to be out on the field again. He wanted to be with his friends.

Pedro and Odete came to see him every day. Maria did not come because she was afraid of hospitals. Fernanda came twice, but she did not come again.

One day Pedro was busy at work. He was not able to come to the hospital and Odete came alone.

'Where's Fernanda?' Palito asked Odete. 'I haven't seen her for more than two weeks.'

'She's busy,' replied Odete. 'But she always asks about you.'

'She's always busy now,' said Palito.

'Fernanda has entered a beauty contest,' said Odete suddenly.

'A *what?*' asked Palito in surprise.

'A beauty contest,' said Odete again. 'You'll be able to see her on television. Perhaps she'll win a prize.'

'Fernanda in a beauty contest!' repeated Palito. 'What will she do next?'

'She wants to become a film star,' said Odete.

'I'll watch her on television,' said Palito. 'Perhaps she'll win first prize.'

Odete and Palito laughed together, but they both felt sad. Fernanda was moving far away from them and from the family.

Chico also came to see Palito most days. One day, Chico met the specialist at the hospital.

'How are Palito's legs now?' Chico asked.

'Fine,' replied the doctor. 'He's doing well. But it's going to take a long time. He'll be in hospital for at least three months.'

Chico told this to Palito.

'Three months,' said Palito. 'I'll be mad in three months. I'll never play football again.'

Chico laughed, but Palito was very worried. He was becoming more bored and more impatient. Antonio was training with the Brazilian team and he was lying in a hospital bed.

On the evening of the beauty contest, Palito watched Fernanda on television. He did not know her at first. She looked very, very beautiful.

Fernanda won third prize in the contest. Palito was angry. Why hadn't she won first prize? The judges were blind. Palito was also sad. Fernanda was gone from him for ever.

A few days after the beauty contest, Fernanda visited Palito in hospital. She had some news for Palito.

'I've got a part in a film,' she told him. 'I'm going to be a film star. I'm leaving for Rio tomorrow.'

'What do Mum and Dad think?' Palito asked.

'They don't want me to go,' replied Fernanda, 'but they can't stop me. Life in Rio is different. I'll have lots of friends there and I'll be happy.'

Fernanda visited Palito in hospital.

'What about you and me?' asked Palito.

'Aunt Maria once wanted us to get married,' said Fernanda. 'But we have both changed. You're now a famous footballer. And I'm going to be a film star. I'm sorry, Palito. It's all over. I'm going to Rio tomorrow.'

Fernanda said goodbye and hurried out of the hospital. The next day she left for Rio.

10

More Trouble

After eight weeks, the plaster was taken from Palito's legs. Palito watched with interest. His legs had turned completely white, but now they looked much straighter.

At last Palito got out of bed. He tried to stand up, but he nearly fell over. He was not able to stand alone at first. A nurse helped him or he held on to something.

Slowly Palito learnt to walk again. He did exercises and his legs became stronger. After two weeks, Palito was able to walk down the hospital steps. Pedro held one arm and Chico held the other. They helped Palito into a car and drove him home.

Palito had to go back to the hospital every day for many weeks. He did special exercises and the doctor watched his legs carefully.

'When can I play football again?' Palito often asked the doctor.

Every time the doctor gave the same reply.

'Soon,' he said.

After five weeks, Palito's legs were X-rayed once more. This time the doctor was satisfied. The bones in Palito's legs had healed perfectly.

'You can start training again,' the doctor told him. 'But don't do too much at first. Begin with half an hour every day.'

Palito was back on the field again! Antonio and Waldir joked about his legs.

'Look at his new legs!' they shouted. 'The supporters

Slowly Palito learnt to walk again.

won't know him. They'll think that the team has a new player.'

Palito was happy again and he began to forget his troubles.

I'll play for Brazil next year, he told himself.

But Palito's happiness did not last for long. His legs were straight and strong, but he could not run fast. His old skills were gone.

'Don't worry,' Chico told him. 'You have new legs now. You must learn to use them properly.'

One day after training, Palito was alone in the dressing room. He was feeling miserable. Chico came in.

'Cheer up,' said Chico when he saw Palito. 'I've got some news for you. You're going to play again.'

Palito sat up immediately. 'That's great.'

'I want you to play for the second team next Sunday,' said Chico.

'For the second team?'

'Yes, for the second team,' replied Chico. 'You need a lot more practice. You'll play in the first team as soon as you're ready.'

Palito played very badly. He had lost all his old skills. The defenders stopped him easily and he did not get one pass through to the strikers. The second team lost the game three goals to one. And their one goal was scored from a pass on the left wing.

'You need much more practice,' Chico told Palito after the game. 'Continue with your exercises. Train harder.'

'And when can I play again?' asked Palito.

'When you're ready.'

I'll never be ready, Palito told himself. I'll never play football again.

Palito began to drink a lot. At night, he went out alone to bars in the city. He often met White Star supporters who were pleased to sit and drink with him. They talked about the games that Palito had played. Palito was still their hero. Palito enjoyed getting drunk with his fans.

In the mornings, Palito stayed in bed late. He arrived late for training. Some days he did not appear at all. Pedro, Maria and Odete were worried. They argued with him and shouted at him.

'You'll lose your job,' Maria told him many times. And she was nearly right.

I'll have to look for another young player, Chico was thinking. Perhaps Palito will never play football again.

11

Waldir's Advice

One day, White Star held a big party. Antonio had come from Buenos Aires. He had played for Brazil against Argentina. In the last minute of the game, Antonio had scored the winning goal. He had come back a hero.

Palito did not want to go to the party. He was jealous of Antonio's success. Odete was going to the party with Waldir. She asked Palito to go too. There was an argument, but finally Palito agreed to go.

During the party, Odete watched Palito carefully. After a while, she saw that he was drinking too much. Odete asked him to go for a walk with her in the garden. Palito agreed, but very unwillingly.

'You're drinking too much again,' she told him.

'That's my business,' said Palito.

'And it's our business too,' replied Odete. 'And Chico's. We all want you to play again for the first team. And Dad wants to see you playing for Brazil one day – like Antonio.'

'Mind your own business,' shouted Palito.

'Hi, there, Palito,' said a voice. 'What are you shouting about?'

It was Waldir. He had come to find Odete. He wanted to dance with her.

'It's not your business, either,' shouted Palito. 'You can all go to hell.'

'Listen a moment . . .' Waldir began.

Palito raised his fists and turned angrily towards Waldir. But Waldir caught Palito's shoulders with his strong hands. He forced Palito to sit down on a wooden seat. When he was

sitting quietly, Waldir spoke to him.

'You feel sorry for yourself,' said Waldir. 'But you've no reason to feel miserable. Your legs are better. They're straight and strong. Isn't that true?'

There was a long silence.

'Yes, that's true,' Palito said slowly. 'But I can't use my legs any more. I wish I had my old, twisted legs back again.'

'You have new legs now,' replied Waldir. 'You need more time to get used to them.'

'What can I do?' said Palito. 'I've tried everything. It's no good.'

'You haven't tried hard enough,' was Waldir's reply. 'Work and train harder. You can still be a great footballer again.'

'And Dad still wants to see you playing for Brazil one day,' added Odete. 'Why don't you try harder? Show him that you can do it!'

Odete and Waldir waited for Palito's reply.

'OK,' he said at last. 'I'll try once again and I'll try harder this time.'

Odete and Waldir did not go back to the party. They went back home with Palito and Palito went straight to bed.

Palito was out on the field at seven o'clock the next morning. He was never late for training again.

12

Tonoko's Gymnasium

Next day at work, Odete had an idea. Small children with weak bones and twisted legs were often brought to Dr Silveira. He was good at treating these children. Odete told the doctor about Palito's trouble. Dr Silveira was immediately interested. He went with Odete to meet Chico and the team doctor.

They told him about Palito's legs and the operation.

'Small children often have this operation,' said Dr Silveira. 'They learn to use their new legs very quickly. But it is more difficult for an older person. And it is even more difficult for a sportsman.'

'Can we do anything for Palito?' asked Chico.

'There is one man in São Paulo who can help him,' replied the doctor. 'Senhor Tonoko. He's Japanese. He owns a gymnasium and he gives special training for sportsmen.'

'Let's speak to Palito, then,' said Chico.

Chico and Dr Silveira talked to Palito and he agreed to visit the Japanese gymnasium.

They went together and met Senhor Tonoko. In the gymnasium, lots of people were training and doing all kinds of exercises.

Senhor Tonoko asked Palito to run round the gymnasium. He asked Palito to dance by himself. Then he asked him to walk along a narrow bar. Palito found this very difficult.

'Is there any hope?' asked Chico when Senhor Tonoko had finished.

'Of course there's hope,' replied Tonoko. 'Palito has

Then Senhor Tonoko asked him to walk along a narrow bar.

new legs and his body is not used to them. It's more difficult for him because he's a sportsman. He wants to use these new legs like his old legs. But this will take time.'

'How long?' asked Palito immediately.

'You'll have to do exercises here every evening,' replied Tonoko. 'It will be hard work for you, but after three months you'll be able to play first-class football again.'

Palito was now training harder than ever. In the morning, he was on the field with the team. And every evening he went to Senhor Tonoko's gymnasium.

In the gymnasium, Palito did simple exercises for the first two weeks. He ran round and jumped up and down. He walked along the narrow bar again and again. Then Palito learnt to box and to play basketball. He learnt once again to move quickly and unexpectedly.

Ten weeks later, Senhor Tonoko surprised all Palito's friends. They were all invited to the gymnasium to watch a boxing match. Odete went with her father and Waldir; and Chico was there with Dr Silveira.

Palito was one of the boxers. In the ring, Palito danced round his opponent and cleverly kept out of trouble. From time to time, Palito moved unexpectedly and hit his opponent. In the end, the winner was Palito.

After the boxing match, everyone congratulated Palito.

'You can move better than before,' said Chico. 'I want you back in the first team next Sunday. We're not doing very well. We need you there.'

The next Sunday, the loud shout was heard once again in the White Star stadium: 'Pa-li-to . . . Pa-li-to . . .'

Chico and Pedro watched the game together. They were both very nervous because of Palito.

In the ring, Palito danced round his opponent and cleverly kept out of trouble.

The referee blew his whistle and Antonio passed the ball to Palito.

'Look how fast Palito's running,' shouted Pedro. 'No one can catch him! He's centring the ball. There's Antonio! G-oo-al!'

A goal in less than twenty seconds! Palito was back.

13

A Telephone Call

Palito was back in the first team, but the season was nearly over. He played better than ever before. Antonio had already been chosen to play for Brazil. But Palito had come back to football too late in the season.

Palito had learnt to be patient.

'I'll play for Brazil next year,' he told his father.

The season ended and Palito took the family to the seaside for a holiday. The days passed happily. Odete and Palito lay on the beach in the sun. Sometimes they swam in the sea or played games on the sand with other holidaymakers.

Pedro and Maria were happy together. They sat and talked about the old days in Salvador. They were sad sometimes when they remembered Fernanda. She was no longer part of the family. She was living her own life in Rio. But Palito's parents were pleased that their son and Odete were so happy together.

One evening, they watched a football match on television. Brazil was playing against the rest of South America. Antonio was playing and Palito watched with interest. It was not a good game and neither side played very well. The game ended in a nil-nil draw.

All the family laughed when they saw Antonio's face on television. He looked angry because he had not scored a goal.

The next day, Palito was lying out in the sun. Maria called him from the house.

'Telephone,' she shouted. 'It's Chico. He's calling from São Paulo.'

'I've got good news for you,' Chico told Palito on the phone.

'Good news,' said Palito. 'What's happened?'

'Did you see the game on television last night?' asked Chico.

'Yes,' replied Palito. 'It wasn't a very good game.'

'You're right,' said Chico. 'We didn't play well at all. And that's why I'm phoning you. You're wanted in Rio de Janeiro. You're to go there and join the team.'

'Me?' shouted Palito. 'Join the team?'

'Come up to São Paulo tomorrow,' said Chico. 'You can meet me here and we'll fly to Rio.'

'I'll see you tomorrow,' said Palito, and put the phone down.

'Dad! Mum! Odete!' called Palito.

The three of them came running into the room.

'What's happened?' asked Pedro.

'That was Chico on the phone,' replied Palito. 'I'm going with him to Rio. I'm going to play for Brazil!'

'You're going to play for Brazil!' Odete, Maria and Pedro shouted out together.

'That's right,' said Palito. 'And now we must hurry. I'm leaving for São Paulo tomorrow. And you, too, Dad. You're coming with me. You always wanted to see me playing football for Brazil.'

14

A Great Day

A week later, Pedro's dream came true. He sat in the huge Maracaña stadium in Rio de Janeiro and watched his son playing for Brazil.

Odete and Maria were watching Palito too. They saw the game on television. And far away on Gloria in Salvador, the people were listening to the game on the radio.

The match was between Brazil and a strong team from Europe. It was a very hot evening and both teams were hoping for an early goal.

The game began badly for Brazil. In the first seconds, Antonio lost the ball in mid-field and the Europeans moved quickly forward. One pass, then another and another brought the ball close to the Brazilian goal. The Brazilian strikers moved back and tried to help their defenders. They moved too slowly and too late.

The ball was passed to a European striker. He was completely unmarked. He ran into an open space in front of goal and kicked the ball hard. The Brazilian goalkeeper saw the danger, but he moved too slowly. The ball passed to his left and into the corner of the net.

Only a few minutes of the match were gone and Brazil were already losing. Palito had not touched the ball yet!

The crowd was silent. Why had Antonio lost the ball so easily? Why had the European striker not been marked? Palito was asking himself the same questions.

The Europeans had scored the important first goal and now they defended. The Brazilians attacked, but the European defenders marked Antonio and the others closely.

He sat in the huge Maracaña stadium in Rio de Janeiro and watched his son playing for Brazil.

Twice in the first half, Palito showed his skills. Once, he passed three defenders in turn and he made a beautiful pass in front of the European goal. A Brazilian striker was waiting in the middle. He kicked the ball hard, but the goalkeeper saved it well.

In the second half, the Brazilians continued to attack. At half-time their manager had told the players: 'Use the wings more. Use Palito on the right.' It was good advice.

Palito had more chances to use the ball now. The backs kept passing the ball up the right wing. The European team changed their plan as well. Two of their defenders were now marking Palito.

But Brazil's first goal did not come from Palito on the right wing. The Europeans were busy marking Palito. They were not covering the other side of the Brazilian attack. Suddenly the ball was passed to Antonio on the left of the field. He ran a few metres and passed the ball to another Brazilian player. Antonio kept running and the ball came back to him in front of the goal. A strong shot from Antonio's left foot put the ball into the net. Brazil 1, Europe 1.

A great roar filled the Maracaña stadium. Brazil was now playing good, exciting football and their supporters were enjoying themselves. The crowd danced up and down and shouted madly.

But there was very little time left. Fifteen minutes. Ten minutes. Where was the winning goal? Who was going to score it? The Brazilian supporters knew the answer: 'Pa-li-to,' they shouted, 'Pa-li-to.' And they were right.

The winning goal was a beauty! Again the ball was in mid-field. The Brazilian players passed it to each other in the middle of the field. Then a long pass came to one of the Brazilian strikers. He stopped the ball, turned quickly and passed it across to the right wing. Palito was waiting. He ran free from a defender and raced up the wing. Another defender, a larger man, moved across to tackle him.

Palito slowed down and stopped. The ball was at his feet. His body bent to the right. Then to the left. The defender did not know which way to turn. He moved forward and Palito cleverly pushed the ball between the player's legs. The defender tried to turn, but Palito was already past him.

Palito saw the space between him and the goalkeeper and kicked the ball with his right foot. It went past the goalkeeper into the top corner of the net.

Another goal for Brazil! And Palito had scored it by himself.

The crowd shouted and danced wildly. The noise was heard clearly on the television and on the radio. Palito's name was heard all over Brazil.

A few minutes later, the final whistle blew. The match was over and Brazil had won. They had beaten the Europeans by two goals to one. Antonio had scored one of the goals and Palito had scored the other.

It was a great day for Palito and for Pedro. And for all the family and Palito's old friends far away in Salvador.

After the game, Pedro hurried through the crowds towards the dressing-rooms. He wanted to congratulate his son. But Palito was not in the dressing-room. Everybody was looking for him, but he had disappeared.

'Where's Palito?' Pedro asked Chico.

'I'm looking for him, too,' replied Chico. 'Everyone wants to congratulate him.'

Palito came into the room. He was wearing his shorts and had not changed.

'Everyone's looking for you,' said Pedro. 'They all want

to congratulate you. Where have you been?'

'I was talking on the telephone,' replied Palito.

'Oh, I understand,' said Pedro. 'You told Maria and Odete about your great game.'

'No,' replied Palito. 'I was talking to Odete about something else.'

Pedro understood immediately and put his arms round his son.

'Congratulations on the game,' he said. 'And congratulations on your choice. Odete will make a wonderful wife.'

15

The Promise is Kept

Six months later, Odete and Palito were married. Fernanda sent them a telegram of congratulations. She could not come to the wedding because she was far away in Mexico. She was making a film there.

Palito now played regularly for Brazil. His name soon became known in stadiums all over South America and Europe.

Pedro still worked for Senhor Castro. He enjoyed driving big, foreign cars and talking to Senhor Castro about football and Palito. And Maria was happy too.

Time passed and Palito became a rich man. But he and Odete were careful with their money. They now had two children of their own.

Odete often visited Dr Silveira at his children's hospital in São Paulo. With Dr Silveira's help, Palito and Odete built a children's hospital in Salvador. It was built on empty ground near Gloria, where Odete and Palito had lived as children.

When Palito was born, the old woman had said: 'This boy will grow up and become famous.'

The name of Palito was now known in many countries all over the world.

'He will give happiness to many people,' the old woman had said.

Many thousands of people enjoyed watching Palito on the football field.

'He will help poor people,' the old woman had told his father.

The children's hospital in Bahia gave help to many poor, sick children.

The old woman had spoken the truth. She had kept her promise.

Points for Understanding

1

1 What was the name of the hill in Salvador where Pedro and Maria lived?
2 Maria was going to have a baby. Why was Pedro worried?
3 What question did Pedro ask the old woman about the baby boy?
4 What was the old woman's promise?
5 What advice did the old woman give to Pedro?

2

1 What was the baby's name?
2 What did the other children call him and why?
3 What was Pedro's new job?
4 Two girls came to live with the family. Why did they come?
5 One of the girls was very pretty; the other was a good student. What were their names?
6 Palito was not a good student. What was he good at?

3

1 What happened to Palito on his fifteenth birthday?
2 Who were 'Corinthians'?
3 What did Palito and his father do every Sunday afternoon?
4 One day, Palito received a letter about a job.
   (a)   Who was the letter from?
   (b)   What was the job?
5 Why did Pedro not want his son to accept the job?
6 Why were the girls surprised at Pedro's words?
7 What advice did Pedro give his son?
8 Did Palito accept his father's advice?
9 'That is the greatest ambition of my life,' Pedro said to Palito. What was Pedro's ambition?

4

1 Who wrote an article about Palito in the newspaper?
2 Pedro brought copies of the newspaper home with him. Why?
3 Everyone on Gloria waited for news. What sort of news?
4 'Take the job with Bahia Central,' some friends told Palito. What was his reply?
5 Who was Chico Perez and what was 'White Star'?
6 Why was Chico Perez coming to Salvador?

5

1 In the match between Corinthians and Recife Rangers:
   (a)   What was the final score?
   (b)   How many goals did Palito score?
2 What happened on Gloria that night?

6

1 Chico Perez asked Palito one question. What was it?
2 What was Palito's reply to Chico?
3 Palito was offered a job. What was the job?
4 Where was the family's new home?
5 What was Pedro's new job?
6 Fernanda, Odete and Maria found new work too. What did they do?
7 Palito made two special new friends. Who were they?
8 Why did Pedro feel so proud?

7

1 Fernanda was becoming successful. What was her new job?
2 In what way had she changed?
3 Who did Odete work for now?
4 Why did Chico Perez worry about Palito?
5 Why did Palito go to the hospital?
6 Did the doctor find anything seriously wrong with Palito?
7 What did the newspapers say about Palito?
8 What happened to Palito in his last game of the season?

1 'What's wrong with Palito's legs?' Chico asked. What was the specialist's reply?
2 What did the specialist plan to do in the operation?
3 'When will I play football again?' Palito asked. What was the specialist's reply?

9

1 Why did Maria not visit Palito in hospital?
2 Why were Odete and Palito sad about Fernanda?
3 Which team was Antonio training with now?
4 Chico spoke to the doctor about Palito's legs. 'He's doing well,' the doctor said. 'But it's going to be a long time.' How long?
5 Palito watched Fernanda on television.
    (a)   Why did he not recognize her at first?
    (b)   Why was he angry?
6 Why was Fernanda going to Rio?
7 How did Pedro and Maria feel about Fernanda's plans?
8 'What about you and me?' Palito asked Fernanda. What did she say?

10

1 When the plaster came off Palito's legs, they looked different. In what two ways were his legs different?
2 Every time Palito asked the doctor about playing football, he got the same reply. What was the doctor's reply?
3 Palito started playing football again, but he was unhappy. Why was he unhappy?
4 Why did he play in the second team and not the first team?
5 Why were Palito's family so worried about him?

11

1 Why did Palito not want to go to the White Star party?
2 'I can't use my legs any more,' Palito told Waldir. What was Waldir's reply?

3 How did the conversation at the party help Palito?
4 Where was Palito at seven o'clock the next morning?

12

1 There was one man in São Paulo who could help Palito. What was his name?
2 Where did Palito go for exercises every evening?
3 Who watched Palito's boxing match?
4 What did Chico say to Palito afterwards?

13

1 Where did Palito take the family for a holiday?
2 'You're wanted in Rio de Janeiro,' Chico told Palito on the phone.
    (a)   Why was Palito wanted in Rio?
    (b)   Who was he going to meet in São Paulo the next day?
    (c)   Who was he going to take with him to São Paulo?

14

1 Who were Brazil playing against in the Maracaña Stadium?
2 How did the game begin for Brazil?
3 What did the Brazilian manager tell his team at half-time?
4 What was the final score?
5 Who scored the Brazilian goals?
6 Who did Palito telephone after the match?
7 'Congratulations on your choice,' Pedro said to Palito. What did he mean?

15

1 The old woman had spoken the truth. She had kept her promise.
    (a)   What three things had she promised?
    (b)   In what way had each promise come true?

Published by Macmillan Heinemann ELT
Between Towns Road, Oxford OX4 3PP
Macmillan Heinemann ELT is an imprint of
Macmillan Publishers Limited
Companies and representatives throughout the world
Heinemann is a registered trademark of Harcourt Education, used under licence.

ISBN 1–405072–77–6
EAN 978-1-405072-77-9

Text © R.L. Scott-Buccleuch 1977, 1992, 1998, 2002, 2005
First published 1977. Reissued 1992

Design and illustration © Macmillan Publishers Limited 1998, 2002, 2005

This edition first published 2005

Illustrated by David Barnett
Original cover template design by Jackie Hill
Cover photography by Photographer's Choice/Getty

Printed in Thailand

2009 2008 2007 2006 2005
10 9 8 7 6 5 4 3 2 1